Understanding XAMPP for Newbies!

John Henderson

DEDICATION

Thanks to my wonderful daughter Heidi, for believing in me.

TABLE OF CONTENTS

1 INTRODUCTION _____ *6*

2 INSTALLING XAMPP _____ *9*

3 XAMPP CONTROL PANEL _____ *12*

4 XAMPP SKYPE CONFLICT _____ *14*

5 THE LOCAL HOST _____ *15*

6 PHPMYADMIN _____ *17*

7 XAMPP FOLDERS _____ *18*

8 SETTING UP YOUR SITE _____ *21*

9 WORKING WITH PHPMYADMIN _____ *25*

10 USING DREAMWEAVER _____ *30*

11 CREATING A MYSQL QUERY _____ *33*

12 RESOLVING PAGE ERRORS _____ *38*

13 CHOOSING A HOSTING SERVER _____ *40*

14 USING FTP _____ *42*

15 BACKING UP YOUR WORK _____ *44*

16 COBIAN BACKUP _____ *46*

17 DUMPTIMER _____ *47*

18 CUTE FTP PRO _____ *49*

19 TOAD FOR MYSQL _____ *51*

21 MAKING XAMPP MORE SECURE _____ *55*

23 XAMPP AND THE INTERNET _____ *60*

24 USING PERL _____ *63*

25 A FINAL NOTE _____ *65*

ACKNOWLEDGMENTS

To the XAMPP development team for making our lives so easy.

1 INTRODUCTION

This handbook covers the XAMPP-win32-1.8.2-0-VC9-installer.exe. Pronounced as 'zampp', XAMPP is the acronym for Cross-platform, Apache, MySQL, PHP and Perl or phpmyadmin. However you want to look at it, phpmyadmin is a later addition to the acronym. I have been using XAMPP since 2004, and it has been a reliable and trustworthy piece of software as well as a great addition to my computer system. I use a Windows XP Pro operating system, but XAMPP works on all Windows operating systems as well as the Apple Macintosh operating system and the Linux operating system, hence the cross-platform initial X.

Initially, it was hard coming to grips with it all, but I soldiered on. I made many, many mistakes by adding additional software to my system which caused conflicts, mayhem and regrets. I had to learn the hard way about Windows Services, what they did, how to add them and how to remove them. I worked through reboot after reboot; most times it was a nightmare and I had to start completely from scratch. Over time, I got to understand what XAMPP was doing and why. With that knowledge, I was able to create huge dynamic MySQL database systems for companies here in the UK.

People now use XAMPP with Joomla!, WordPress, Drupal and many more content management systems (CMS). Working with XAMPP is now much, much easier. There is a ton of XAMPP information on the net to help with solving problems, errors and conflicts that may occur from time to time. This handbook is simply a time-saving guide to understanding XAMPP, what it does and why you, as a PHP and MySQL developer, need to have it. I have also tried to make sure that the book is easy to read so that you can use it for future reference.

What Is A Server?

XAMPP is an Apache Server, packaged with MySQL, PHP, Perl and Phpmyadmin. All these products are 'Open Source', which means they are free to use. If you're hoping to create your own dynamic web pages then you're going to need a local web server. XAMPP is FREE and as long as you use PHP and MySQL for your server code then you're on to a winner. Always install the latest version of XAMPP from the Apache Friends dot org website:

http://www.apachefriends.org/en/XAMPP.html

When you install XAMPP, you are installing an Apache process application, which interprets all the files stored in a pre-determined folder on your computer. Once you place your dynamic HTML web pages inside the folder, you're able to view them through your browser. Also installed is a MySQL process application that is required to create, view and run databases.

The main reason that PHP and MySQL are so popular is because they are free to use. If you develop with Microsoft products, ASP and Microsoft SQL, then you will have to pay Microsoft a license fee. When you decide to host your new dynamic web pages and you use PHP and MySQL you will see how inexpensive the hosting servers are compared to Microsoft Hosted Servers.

XAMPP is for your desktop computer; it allows you to build a fully-fledged dynamic web site on your computer. When you have completed your web site, you will then need to use a hosting company that will allow you to upload your files and database to a compatible PHP and MySQL Server. Only then will your dynamic web site be available to the World Wide Web and your customers.

The process of viewing dynamic data is as follows. You write your web pages using HTML, PHP, MySQL, Javascript and CSS. These pages are stored in the htdocs folder inside the XAMPP folder. When you open your browser and type 'localhost' in the address bar, the Apache server will interpret the pages as PHP, and any MySQL code that is executed will also be read. MySQL will then query the database and display the data on your web page.

I have always used Adobe DreamWeaver to write the php code but there are many other applications that you can use to create and edit your code.It is important that you set up your environment to access the XAMPP files quickly and easily. Even more critical is to back them up on a regular basis. I found that when things did go wrong with XAMPP, I could back up the correct folder, uninstall XAMPP and then reinstall it. Later, I could add my backed up folder to the htdocs folder and I would be up and running in minutes. Phew!

Your computer's security is very important and XAMPP covers that. If you have a single computer or a laptop connected to a router, you're safe using XAMPP just as it is, as no one else will be able to access your system. But, if your computer is connected to other computers, you will need to add extra security to XAMPP to protect your system. I will cover that in a later chapter.

You don't need to know everything that XAMPP is capable of, just the parts that affect you and your dynamic web pages. There are plenty of frequently asked questions (FAQ) and Answers on the Apache Friends web site to help you along. So without further ado, let's begin on your road to dynamic web pages.

2 INSTALLING XAMPP

The first thing you must do is decide where you are going to install XAMPP. You will find yourself popping into the folder on regular occasions, so you really need quick access. It is always a good idea to have a Work folder, as this is where you would keep your work. You need to make sure you have plenty of room on your hard drive as XAMPP takes up quite a lot of room. It is recommended that you install it at the root of drive C:\ containing your Windows and Program Files folders. You can then make short cuts to your desktop for easy access. So now you know where to install XAMPP, go and download the application. Follow the instructions on the download page.

Microsoft Visual C++

XAMPP Version 1.8.2 requires the Microsoft Visual C++ 2008 Redistributable package, found here:

http://www.microsoft.com/en-us/download/details.aspx?id=5582

You may already have the Visual C++ package on your system, so go and examine your Add/Remove programs. If you're not sure, download the Visual C++ package and install it anyway. The Visual C++ package installer will prompt you if you don't need to install it.

Once you have installed the Visual C++ package, select the XAMPP Installer version and not the 'Zip' file version. Once again, follow the on screen instructions precisely. If you have anti-virus software running, you will be prompted if you wish to continue. Click Next until you come to the following screen:

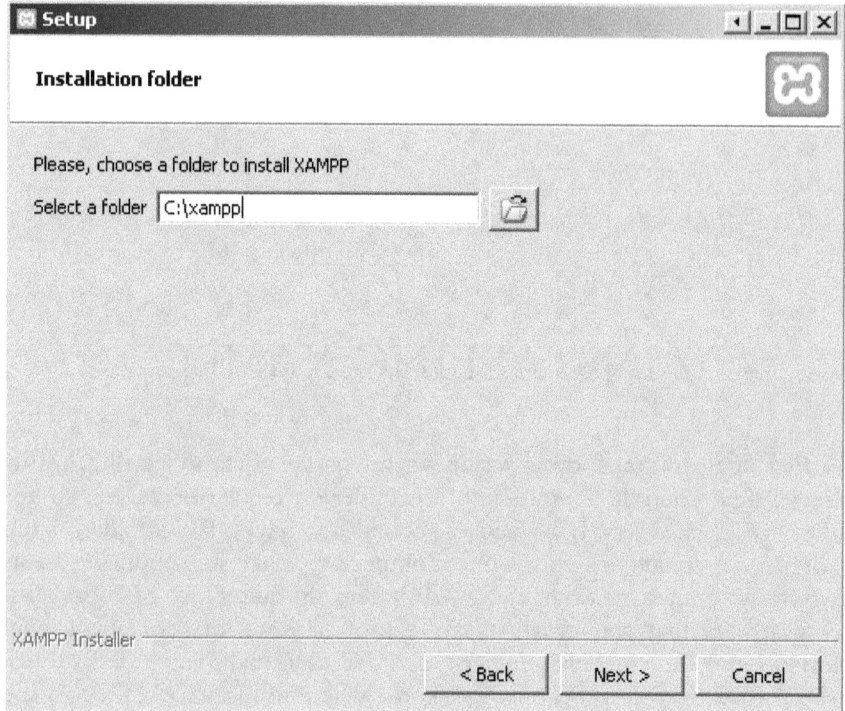

Figure 1

Make sure that your screen looks like Figure 1. XAMPP will create a folder at the root of the C:\ drive. Click Next; the installation may take quite a few minutes, so you will need to be patient.

Once installed, you should receive a Windows Security Alert. Select Unblock to allow Apache to run freely on your system. See Figure 2. You may also see a similar alert asking to Unblock MySQL. Do the same so that MySQL can run freely within your system.

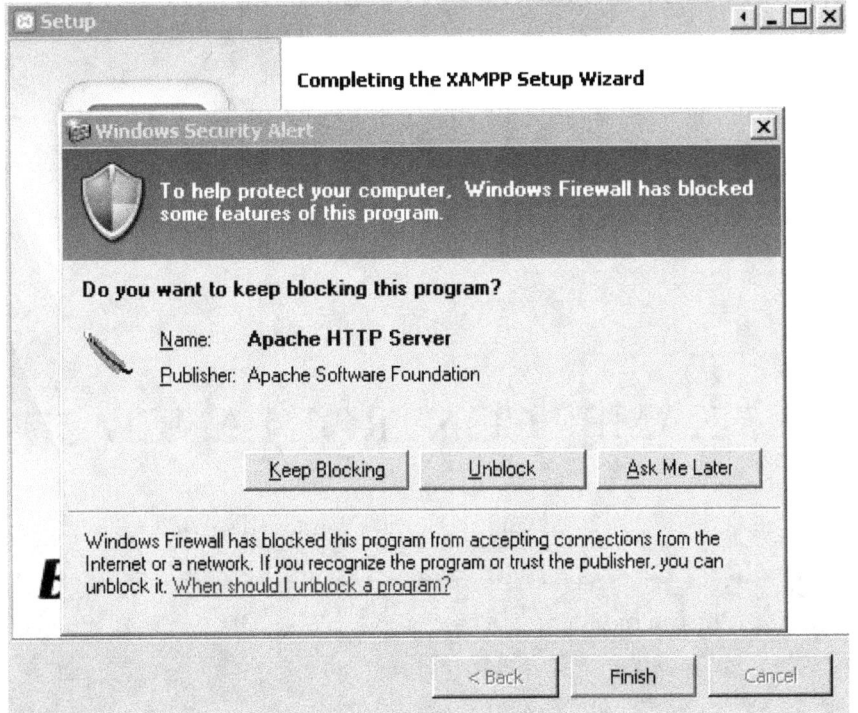

Figure 2

When asked Do you want to start the control panel? Leave the option selected and click Finish.

When prompted, select the Run option to execute the XAMPP control panel.

3 XAMPP CONTROL PANEL

You should now see the following application window displayed.

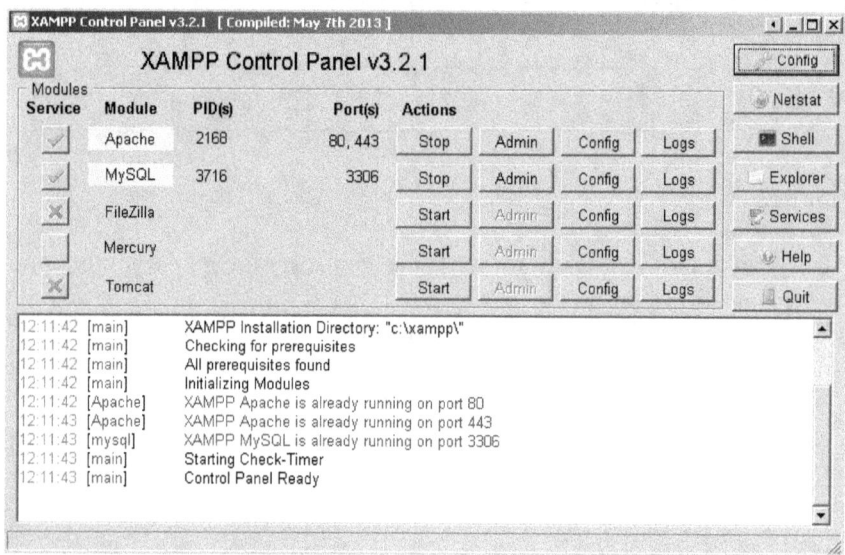

Figure 3

If you have any errors they will appear as red text. You may need to remove applications such as Pando Media Booster, if it is controlling a specific port. Remember to reboot your system after removing a service application. You may also find a port conflict, if you have Skype running in the background. I will explain how to fix this conflict later.

If you open your Services, found in your start menu via Programs/Administrative Tools/Services, you should see something similar to Figure 4. Scroll down to check that MySQL is also installed and running.

The XAMPP control panel can be found in the XAMPP folder, so it's a good idea to have a shortcut on your desktop. The green tick boxes tell you which modules are installed as services. You can uninstall these services just by clicking on the tick boxes. You can also switch these services on or off, depending on the speed of your machine, by clicking Start and Stop. I tend to leave them on and installed as modules, this way you don't have use the control panel at all. When the XAMPP control panel is running you will see an icon displayed in the task bar, near your clock, in the bottom right corner. Simply right clicking on it will tell you which XAMPP services are running. You can also show and hide the control panel with one click.

XAMPP also includes a Java server called Tomcat. This book does not cover the Java programming language. XAMPP also includes Filezilla, an FTP server that allows you to upload and download files from your hosting server. There are many FTP applications available. The FTP software that I use is called Cute FTP Pro, as it is so simple to use. Finally, you will see the mercury email server, which allows you to retrieve and send email from your localhost desktop.

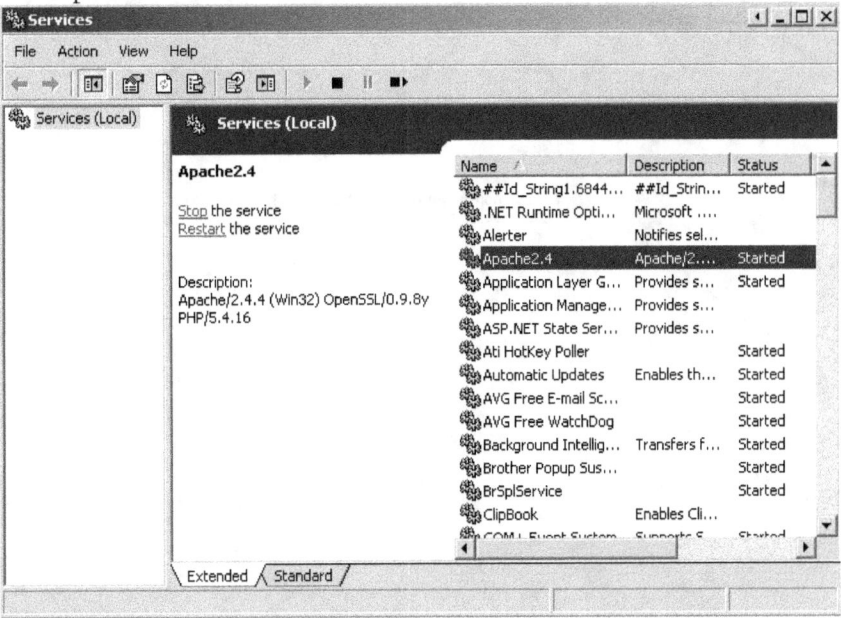

Figure 4

4 XAMPP SKYPE CONFLICT

If you use Skype for your communication system, you will find that the Apache server may no longer run, as there is a conflict with the port settings. Simply go into your Skype Options/Advanced/Connection: and uncheck the box labelled 'Use port 80 and 443 as alternatives for incoming connections'. See Figure 5. Skype will run fine even though your Apache server is still running on port 80.

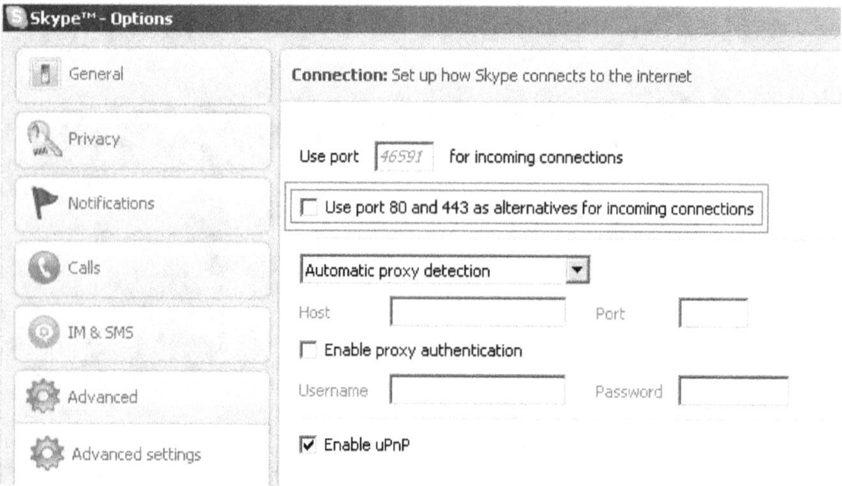

Figure 5

5 THE LOCAL HOST

If all has gone well up to this stage, it's time to check that your browser can see the localhost. This is where your web pages will be visible. In your browser window, type in the word localhost. You should see something similar to Figure 6.

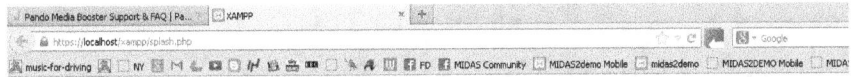

Figure 6

Congratulations! You have installed XAMPP successfully. Now we can run a few tests to ensure there is security and that MySQL is running smoothly. Click on the link entitled English. You will now see a screen similar to Figure 7.

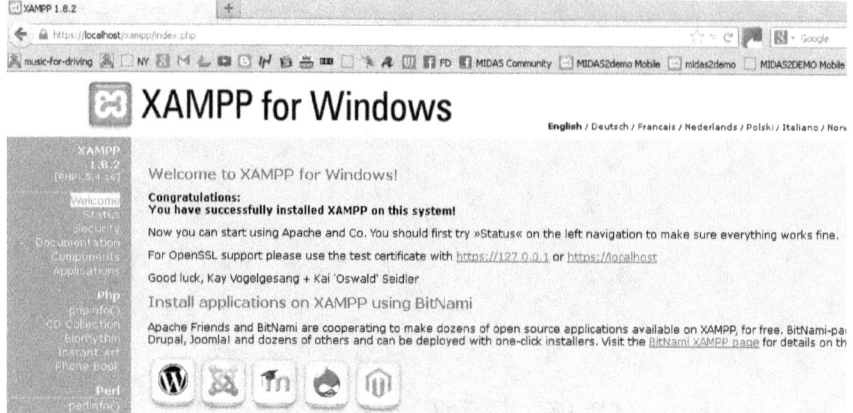

Figure 7

Click on the status link on the left side of the page, this will display all the activated components. These are all that you require to start running dynamic pages. Apache provides you with security options so that outsiders cannot access your system. We will cover this topic later in the book.

Click on the phpinfo link. You should see the PHP version number in the center of the web page see figure 8.

XAMPP for Windows

English / Deutsch / Francais / Nederlands / Polski / Italiano / Norwegia

PHP Version 5.4.16	php

System	Windows NT JOHNSCOMPUTER 5.1 build 2600 (Windows XP Professional Service Pack 3, v.3311) i586
Build Date	Jun 5 2013 20:58:05
Compiler	MSVC9 (Visual C++ 2008)
Architecture	x86
Configure Command	cscript /nologo configure.js "--enable-snapshot-build" "--disable-isapi" "--enable-debug-pack" "--without-mssql" "--without-pdo-mssql" "--without-pi3web" "--with-pdo-oci=C:\php-sdk\oracle\instantclient10\sdk,shared" "--with-oci8=C:\php-sdk\oracle \instantclient10\sdk,shared" "--with-oci8-11g=C:\php-sdk\oracle\instantclient11 \sdk,shared" "--enable-object-out-dir=../obj/" "--enable-com-dotnet=shared" "--with-mcrypt=static" "--disable-static-analyze" "--with-pgo"
Server API	Apache 2.0 Handler

Figure 8

6 PHPMYADMIN

One of the most important programs you will need to help build your dynamic web site is now included with XAMPP. The program is called phpmyadmin, and it allows you to build databases. Click on the phpmyadmin link on the left under the heading Tools'. Phpmyadmin is a very cool browser application. It is a dynamic web browser system, not much different from the system you're hoping to build. See Figure 9.

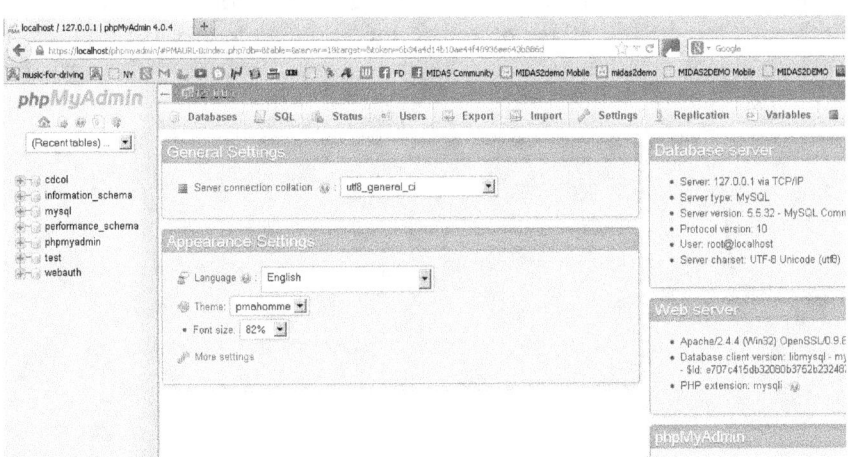

Figure 9

7 XAMPP FOLDERS

Before you start diving in to phpmyadmin, it's important to understand what is going on in your system and where all the components are hidden. See Figure 10. When things go wrong with XAMPP, and they do, it's always helpful to know where to look. The folder in Figure 10 may look overwhelming at first, but once you know where to look, your problems become easier to solve. I have highlighted the folders that you will often need to examine to solve your issues, they are the Apache folder, the htdocs folder, the MySQL folder, the PHP folder and the XAMPP-control.exe application. At the moment everything works fine because you haven't built your dynamic web application yet.

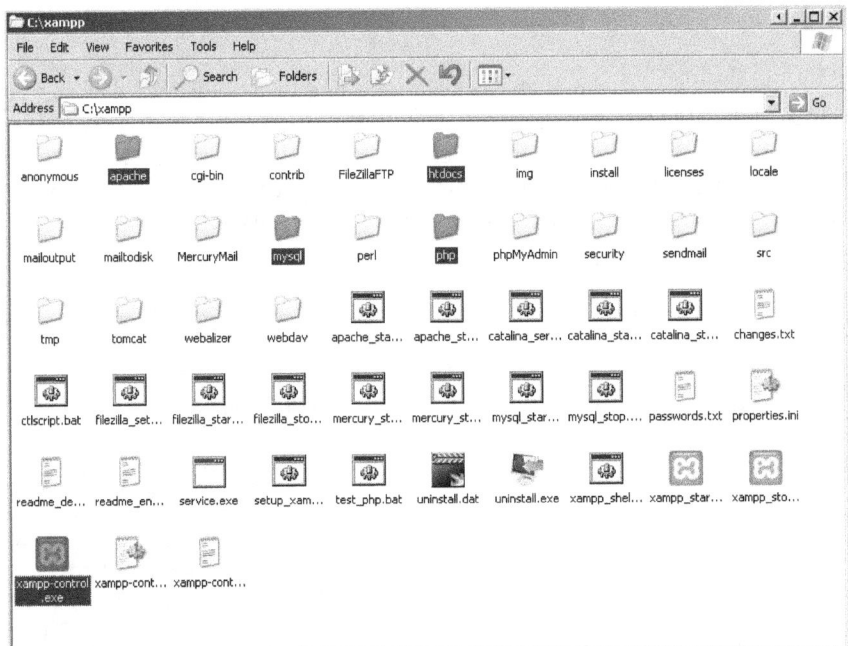

Figure 10

There are two very important folders that you will work with in the XAMPP folder; one is the htdocs folder, and the other is the data folder found inside the MySQL folder.

The htdocs Folder

The htdocs folder is where your site's folder will be stored. It is this folder that Apache uses as the localhost. You will create your web pages and store them in a folder within the htdocs folder. When you enter the address https://localhost into your browser you will see the Welcome to XAMPP for Windows page, and the address bar will change to https://localhost/XAMPP/. If you examine the XAMPP folder within htdocs, you will see all the files that make up the Welcome page, as well as the link pages that are displayed in the left column. In the htdocs folder you will also see a file called index.html. If you enter the following address https://localhost/index.html in to your address bar, you will see the words It Works'. You can now see that by using a folder name for each web site, Apache allows you to build and test multiple web sites.

The data Folder

Inside the MySQL folder is the data folder. The data folder will house your database files. If you look inside the cdcol folder you should see a number of files that are all associated with the cdcol database. See Figure 11. The more data that you enter into the cdcol database the larger the file sizes become. As you build your database in the future it is the files contained in this folder that you will learn to back up regularly.

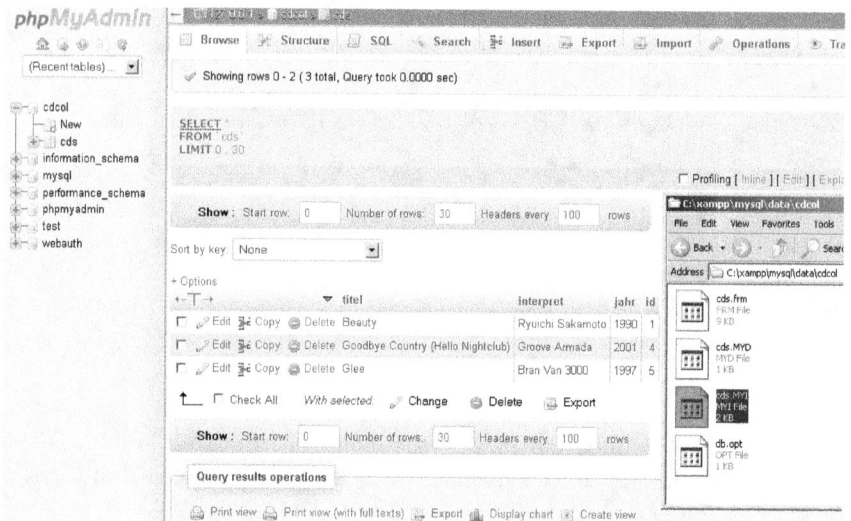

Figure 11

Always remember to back up your 'htdocs' folder and your database folder.

8 SETTING UP YOUR SITE

If you decide to use Adobe DreamWeaver to create your dynamic web site, you will be asked to locate your local root folder. You can create this root folder on your desktop for easy access to your working folder. You will also be asked to locate your remote folder; this is usually located on your online hosting server. Chances are you don't have a hosting server provider as yet. It's best to set your testing server and remote server to the XAMPP htdocs folder, to save any confusion. Ensure the root folder and remote/testing folder always has the same name. DreamWeaver will automatically synchronise files between both folders, so you won't have to.

Most of your files will end with the prefix .php, as this is the language that you will use to access your database. PHP is known as server-side code, which means it is executed on the server and not on the local desktop. Javascript code and Flash code are executed on your desktop, this means your browser interprets the code and executes it. PHP code may be executed by a click of the button but the code is executed on the server. So, if you examine a PHP file in a web browser you will not see any PHP code within the file.

When you test your php files within the XAMPP environment via your browser and the local host, your PHP code is checked for errors. You can manually set the level of errors you want to see by changing the details of the PHP.ini file. If you open the PHP.ini file, which you can find inside XAMPP/PHP/, you should see the Error Level Constants. XAMPP makes it pretty easy to adjust the Constants to suit your error level requirements. Do remember that if you make any changes to the file, you will need to restart the Apache server to include the new changes. For in-depth details view the documentation provided with XAMPP on your localhost.

Error Level Constants

```
php.ini - Notepad
File  Edit  Format  View  Help
;   development servers and development settings are for.
;   Note: The php.ini-development file has this setting as E_ALL | E_STRICT. This
;   means it pretty much reports everything which is exactly what you want during
;   development and early testing.
;
;   Error Level Constants:
;   E_ALL             - All errors and warnings (includes E_STRICT as of PHP 6.0.0)
;   E_ERROR           - fatal run-time errors
;   E_RECOVERABLE_ERROR  - almost fatal run-time errors
;   E_WARNING         - run-time warnings (non-fatal errors)
;   E_PARSE           - compile-time parse errors
;   E_NOTICE          - run-time notices (these are warnings which often result
;                       from a bug in your code, but it's possible that it was
;                       intentional (e.g., using an uninitialized variable and
;                       relying on the fact it's automatically initialized to an
;                       empty string)
;   E_STRICT          - run-time notices, enable to have PHP suggest changes
;                       to your code which will ensure the best interoperability
;                       and forward compatibility of your code
;   E_CORE_ERROR      - fatal errors that occur during PHP's initial startup
;   E_CORE_WARNING    - warnings (non-fatal errors) that occur during PHP's
;                       initial startup
;   E_COMPILE_ERROR   - fatal compile-time errors
;   E_COMPILE_WARNING - compile-time warnings (non-fatal errors)
;   E_USER_ERROR      - user-generated error message
;   E_USER_WARNING    - user-generated warning message
;   E_USER_NOTICE     - user-generated notice message
;   E_DEPRECATED      - warn about code that will not work in future versions
;                       of PHP
;   E_USER_DEPRECATED - user-generated deprecation warnings
;
;   Common Values:
;     E_ALL (Show all errors, warnings and notices including coding standards.)
;     E_ALL & ~E_NOTICE  (Show all errors, except for notices)
;     E_ALL & ~E_NOTICE & ~E_STRICT  (Show all errors, except for notices and coding standards warnings.)
;     E_COMPILE_ERROR|E_RECOVERABLE_ERROR|E_ERROR|E_CORE_ERROR  (Show only errors)
;   Default Value: E_ALL & ~E_NOTICE & ~E_STRICT & ~E_DEPRECATED
```

Service Logs

In the XAMPP/apache/logs/ folder you will find log files. These are files that Apache writes to while it is running. These log files are helpful in assisting with tracking problems and errors whilst building your web site.

Access Log

"http://localhost/phpmyadmin/index.php?db=midas0001&token=f07b176c
d240742b3f7bcb7e40f35bd6" "Mozilla/5.0 (Windows NT 5.1; rv:20.0)
Gecko/20100101 Firefox/20.0"
127.0.0.1 - - [03/Jul/2013:08:54:36 +0100] "GET
/phpmyadmin/themes/pmahomme/img/arrow_ltr.png HTTP/1.1" 200 139
"http://localhost/phpmyadmin/db_structure.php?token=f07b176cd240742b
3f7bcb7e40f35bd6&db=midas0001" "Mozilla/5.0 (Windows NT 5.1; rv:20.0)
Gecko/20100101 Firefox/20.0"
127.0.0.1 - - [03/Jul/2013:09:14:03 +0100] "GET / HTTP/1.1" 302 - "-"
"Mozilla/5.0 (Windows NT 5.1; rv:20.0) Gecko/20100101 Firefox/20.0"
127.0.0.1 - - [03/Jul/2013:09:14:03 +0100] "GET /XAMPP/ HTTP/1.1"
200 594 "-" "Mozilla/5.0 (Windows NT 5.1; rv:20.0) Gecko/20100101
Firefox/20.0"
127.0.0.1 - - [03/Jul/2013:09:14:03 +0100] "GET /XAMPP/head.php
HTTP/1.1" 200 1393 "https://localhost/XAMPP/" "Mozilla/5.0 (Windows
NT 5.1; rv:20.0) Gecko/20100101 Firefox/20.0"

127.0.0.1 - - [03/Jul/2013:09:14:03 +0100] "GET /XAMPP/start.php
HTTP/1.1" 200 1067 "https://localhost/XAMPP/" "Mozilla/5.0 (Windows
NT 5.1; rv:20.0) Gecko/20100101 Firefox/20.0"
127.0.0.1 - - [03/Jul/2013:09:14:03 +0100] "GET /XAMPP/navi.php
HTTP/1.1" 200 3921 "https://localhost/XAMPP/" "Mozilla/5.0 (Windows
NT 5.1; rv:20.0) Gecko/20100101 Firefox/20.0"
127.0.0.1 - - [03/Jul/2013:09:21:08 +0100] "POST
/CFIDE/main/ide.cfm?CFSRV=IDE&ACTION=IDE_DEFAULT
HTTP/1.1" 404 1052 "-" "MMHttp (Windows; Version:9.0)"
127.0.0.1 - - [03/Jul/2013:09:38:45 +0100] "POST
/CFIDE/main/ide.cfm?CFSRV=IDE&ACTION=IDE_DEFAULT
HTTP/1.1" 404 1052 "-" "MMHttp (Windows; Version:9.0)"

Error Log

[Thu Jul 04 22:42:00.234375 2013] [mpm_winnt:notice] [pid 4148:tid 1884]
AH00364: Child: All worker threads have exited.
[Thu Jul 04 22:42:00.281250 2013] [mpm_winnt:notice] [pid 168:tid 284]
AH00430: Parent: Child process exited successfully.
[Fri Jul 05 07:54:18.375000 2013] [ssl:warn] [pid 780:tid 272] AH01873: Init:
Session Cache is not configured [hint: SSLSessionCache]
[Fri Jul 05 07:54:18.953125 2013] [mpm_winnt:notice] [pid 780:tid 272]
AH00455: Apache/2.4.3 (Win32) OpenSSL/1.0.1c PHP/5.4.7 configured --
resuming normal operations
[Fri Jul 05 07:54:18.968750 2013] [mpm_winnt:notice] [pid 780:tid 272]
AH00456: Server built: Aug 18 2012 12:41:37
[Fri Jul 05 07:54:18.968750 2013] [core:notice] [pid 780:tid 272] AH00094:
Command line: 'm:\\XAMPP\\apache\\bin\\httpd.exe -d
M:/XAMPP/apache'
[Fri Jul 05 07:54:18.984375 2013] [mpm_winnt:notice] [pid 780:tid 272]
AH00418: Parent: Created child process 1272
[Fri Jul 05 07:54:20.265625 2013] [ssl:warn] [pid 1272:tid 1884] AH01873:
Init: Session Cache is not configured [hint: SSLSessionCache]
[Fri Jul 05 07:54:20.390625 2013] [mpm_winnt:notice] [pid 1272:tid 1884]
AH00354: Child: Starting 150 worker threads.

Apache has an additional file that contains configuration settings and the server instructions. This is called the httpd.conf file and is found in the XAMPP/apache/conf folder. In this file you can set the server type, server root directory, the log file names and many other commands. On installation, XAMPP will set up all these files automatically and you should have very little reason to change them.

9 WORKING WITH PHPMYADMIN

Phpmyadmin is a descriptor for, PHP, MySQL, and ADMIN.

PHP Stands for Hypertext Preprocessor; it can create web pages and has the ability to access MySQL databases.

MySQL is a relational database management system (RDBMS). It runs as a server on your system, just like Apache, and requires the Structured Query Language to access data. There are many commercial SQL products available on the net, but MySQL is by far the most popular simply because it is free, if not used commercially. MySQL is owned by the Oracle Corporation.

The word ADMIN describes what you can do with the phpmyadmin application.

Phpmyadmin was created using PHP to administrate MySQL databases. There are many applications on the web to help you administer your database, some are commercial products that are quite expensive and some thankfully are free. Phpmyadmin is included with Apache and you don't even have to set it up as it works straight out of the box.
Phpmyadmin is where you will create, edit and query your databases. Databases can contain one or more tables and these tables can contain multiple rows, with multiple columns. When you query or search a table it will display all the matching rows. A row will contain at least one field or column.

If you imagine that your database is a room, and inside that room there are a number of filing cabinets (tables) and inside each filing cabinet there are hundreds of files (rows). Each file will contain details of the customers name and address (columns) as well as additional information. So for example a large utility company may have ten rooms, one for customers, one for invoices, one for contractors, one for suppliers, one for data aggregators etc. You can see where this is going. So to search for information on a particular customer, we need to know which room to start with and then work out which filling cabinet to examine until we find the correct customer.

If On Saturday, we want to send a meter reader to a number of customer's properties so that we can read their water meters, we need to find a way to link the two together. Now, we could just simply print out a list and give it to the aggregator and have him go on his merry way. But it would be helpful to know every time I view a customer's details I can also see who last read the meter. If I know who read the meters, then that would allow me to see how many meters the meter reader has read that day. I could also count all the meter readers employed by the company, and the number of meters they read each day; We now have an idea of the meter reader's workload for the whole day. If we have an Invoice table we could also see how many invoices the customer has paid and when the next invoice is due to be sent.

Using MySQL

Using a relational database like MySQL allows you to connect tables to tables. In MySQL the query is known as a Join. But before we can make the join, we have to have a field in both tables that are identical. If we create a simple table called customers, the first field to be created will also be a primary key. This will also be an auto incrementing number that will be used to join the tables together. Each time you create a new customer, the primary key number will be incremented. So we could call this field the 'customerid', as we know that it will always be unique.

Customer Database		
CustomerID	First Name	Last Name
1	Bill	Johnson
2	Ted	Smith
3	William	Jackson

We can create another table now, that we will call invoices and this again will have an auto incrementing number, we can call 'invoiceid'. But we also want to tie in the correct customer to the correct invoice. If we look at the table, we can see the relationship between the two tables. We can see for example William Jackson has paid 2 Invoices, where as Bill Johnson has not paid his invoice yet.

Customer Invoices			
InvoiceID	CustomerID	Date_Sent	Paid
1	2	20/12/2012	Yes
2	1	20/12/2012	No
3	3	20/12/2012	Yes
4	3	20/11/2012	Yes

Relationships are an integral part of any dynamic system and phpmyadmin includes a relational designer to assist you with building your database. See figure 12.

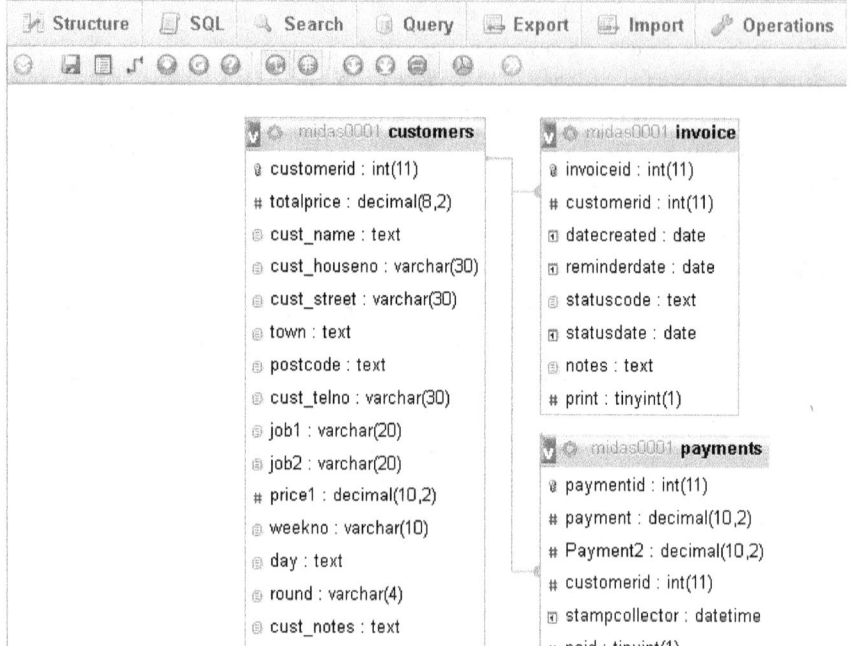

Figure 12

Before you add any MySQL query code to a web page you need to be able to test it. Phpmyadmin allows you to do this very simply. When you click on the SQL tab a field is displayed for you to add your query code. If your code is correct phpmyadmin will display the found dataset. The SQL query code you enter can be very simple or very complex. The code (see Figure 13) is requesting all the data contained in the customer's table. The ORDER BY and LIMIT were added by phpmyadmin.

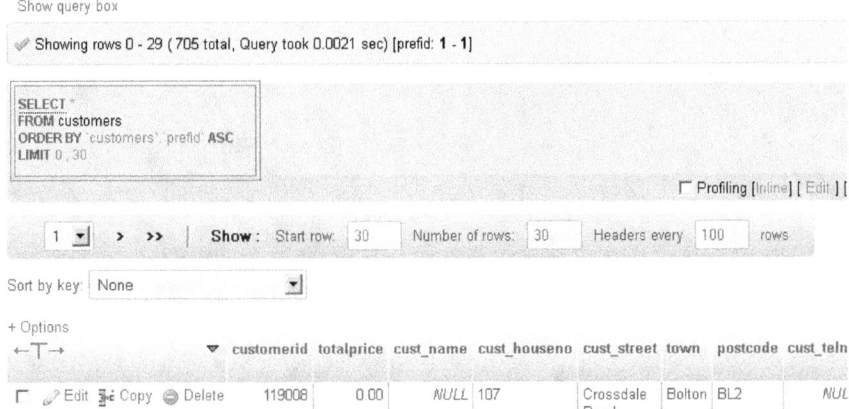

Figure 13

Phpmyadmin will even help you to get started building queries by clicking on the query tab. There are many examples of MySQL code found on the web to help you get started with your MySQL queries. Don't be afraid to try them.

There may be times when you have to export your data or even import your data. Phpmyadmin allows you to export a whole database, a table, or even a query from a table. You can export the structure of the database, the data from the database or even both; In other words, duplicate the database. MySQL lets you make numerous copies of your database so you can use them for testing. There really isn't anything that phpmyadmin can't do regarding MySQL databases. It will take time to get proficient with it, but it will be time well spent. You will need to understand how to manage your growing database and how to improve its speed and efficiency. Learn how to use indexes in your tables to ensure your users can find data as quickly as possible. Your database table could end up storing thousands upon thousands of bits of data; so indexing a regularly used column will help to save the user time and frustration.

Now we need to understand how to connect your web files to your database, run queries from your web page by clicking on buttons and finally, display the results in tables on the web page.

10 USING DREAMWEAVER

I use DreamWeaver to develop my PHP pages. It allows me to make the connections to the XAMPP server as well as connect to MySQL. DreamWeaver also creates the connection file that will allow your pages to access your MySQL database. This file is important, as you will use this file when you upload your pages to your online host.

When you set up your site in DreamWeaver, the first thing you will have to do is set up your 'Site Definition'. For the Local Info we point all our directories to the local host site (root folder) you saved on your desktop, remember? As you create files or add files to the localhost folder, DreamWeaver will add them to the XAMPP\htdocs folder automatically. See Figure 14.

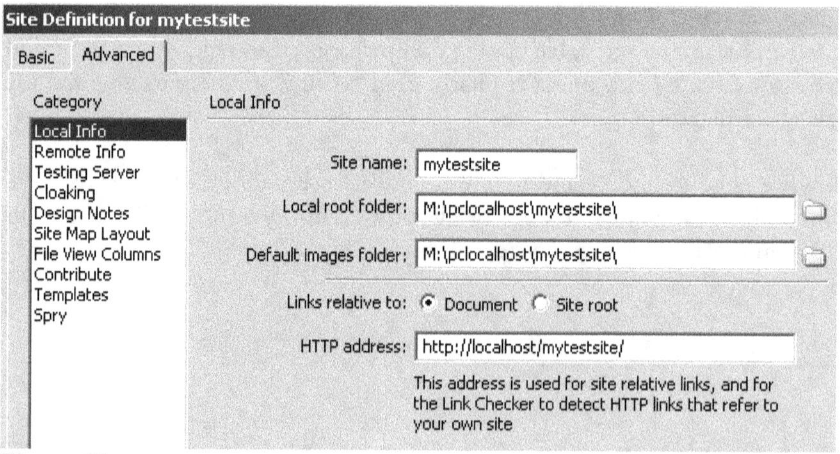

Figure 14

We can see for the 'Testing Server' in Figure 15 that the server model is 'PHP MySQL' and the access is set to local network. The testing server folder is XAMPP\htdocs\mysite\. DreamWeaver is now able to save files that you create and edit into your testing server folder.

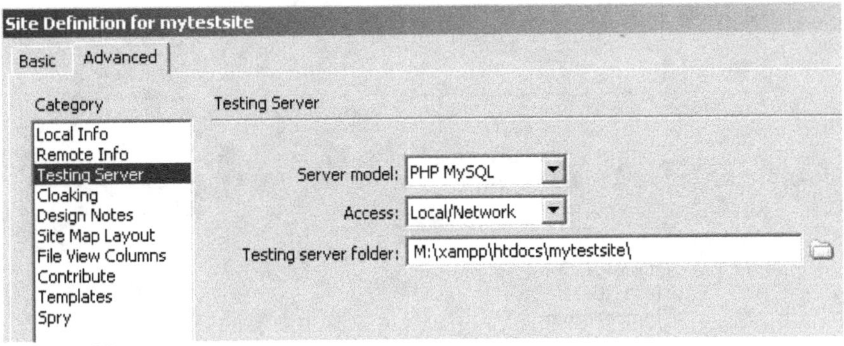

Site Definition for mytestsite

Basic | Advanced

Category | Testing Server

Local Info
Remote Info
Testing Server
Cloaking
Design Notes
Site Map Layout
File View Columns
Contribute
Templates
Spry

Server model: PHP MySQL

Access: Local/Network

Testing server folder: M:\xampp\htdocs\mytestsite\

Figure 15

Once you have set up your 'Site Definition' you need to create a new file, ensuring that the page type is PHP. DreamWeaver will now allow you to connect to a MySQL database. See Figure 16. You will need to give it a connection name. The MySQL server is on the local host and the user name of the MySQL database is 'root'. No passwords have been set as you are the only one using the system. Finally click on the select button and you should see a list of the MySQL databases available. If you have a connection error, you will need to check the XAMPP control panel and ensure that Apache and MySQL are running. Go over your 'Site Definitions' to make sure they are all correct.

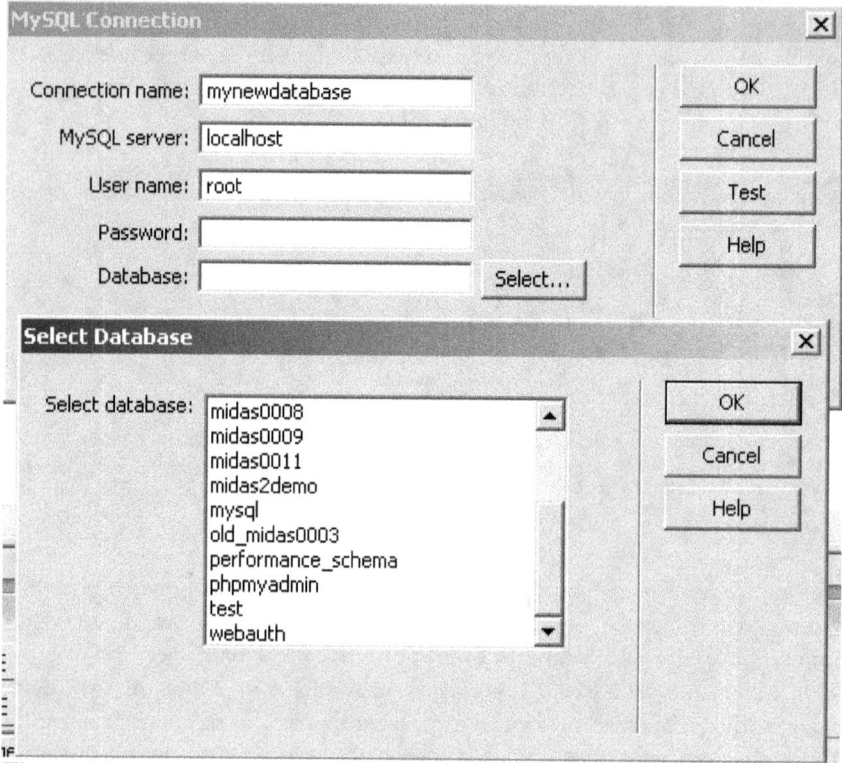

Figure 16

Once you have selected your database, DreamWeaver will have created your connection file, which can be found in the Connections folder.

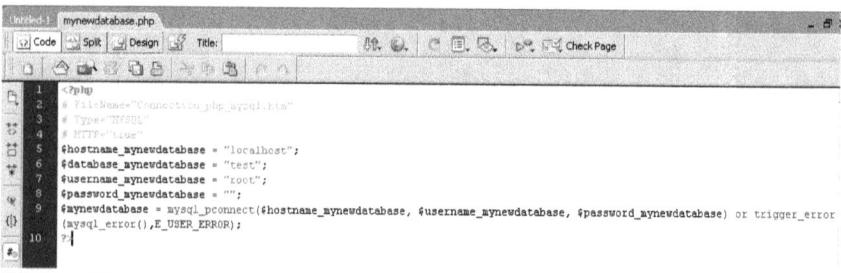

Figure 17

These are the same details (Figure 17) that you entered in Figure 16. When you need to test your files on line, you will need to create a copy of the connection file and edit it.

11 CREATING A MYSQL QUERY

You can now start to create your web site with DreamWeaver making sure each new file is a PHP file. DreamWeaver will add the following PHP code to all your new files:

```php
<?php require_once('../Connections/mynewdatabase.php'); ?>
```

This ensures that all the PHP files will have access to your database. DreamWeaver cleverly allows you to create simple MySQL code by selecting from drop down boxes. I have selected a database that contains plenty of data to provide examples. See Figure 18. The name Recordset1 has been inserted by DreamWeaver, you should always rename this to express what your code is actually doing. For example Recordsetinvoices or Recordsetemployees or recordsetgraphics, etc. This will make things easier to understand when you have to revisit the page at a later date. The connection will default to your connection that you made earlier. The table drop down list will display all the tables held in your database. The columns are the fields you will have created in each table within your database. I have selected the columns that I want to display on my page. The Filter is the column that will be searched. I am asking to search for any record where the cust_houseno = 12 and I want to view the list in ascending order.

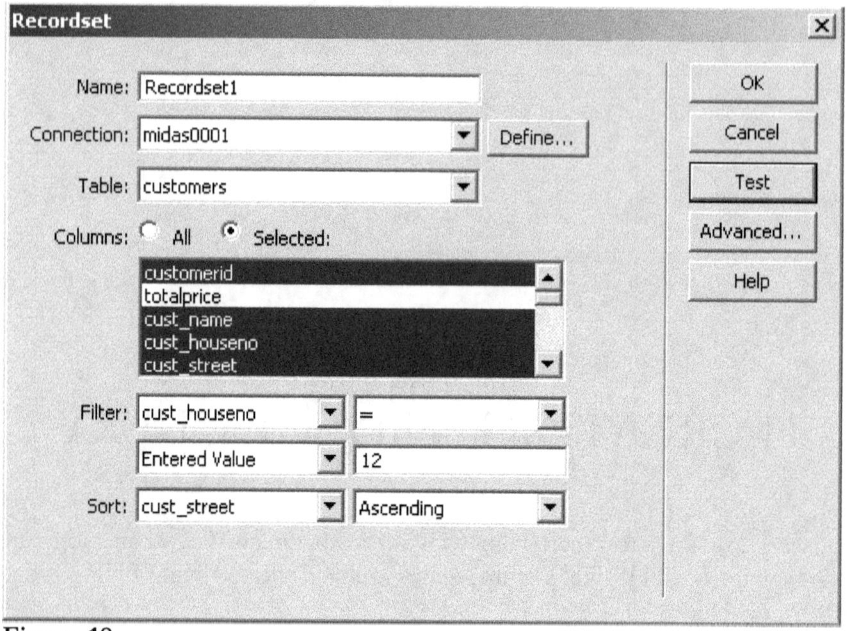

Figure 18

I can now click on 'Test' and see the results of my query. See Figure 19. DreamWeaver has successfully run the MySQL code without any errors and displays the data in a list format. This is the data that I want reproducing in my web page.

Test SQL Statement

R...	custo...	c...	c...	cust_street
1	15450...		12	Berkleigh Walk
2	8028458		12	Brantfell Close
3	16368...		12	Cronel Drive
4	15737...		12	Highwood close
5	15208...		12	Kings Fold Close
6	8028605		12	Lenham Gardens
7	8028574		12	Mendip Drive
8	16368...		12	Sandhurst Drive
9	8028310		12	Skelton Grove
10	8028505		12	Slaidburn Avenue
11	241922		12	Slimbridge Drive
12	8028563		12	Somerton Road
13	8028494		12	Swinside Road
14	8028342		12	Tetbury Drive

Figure 19

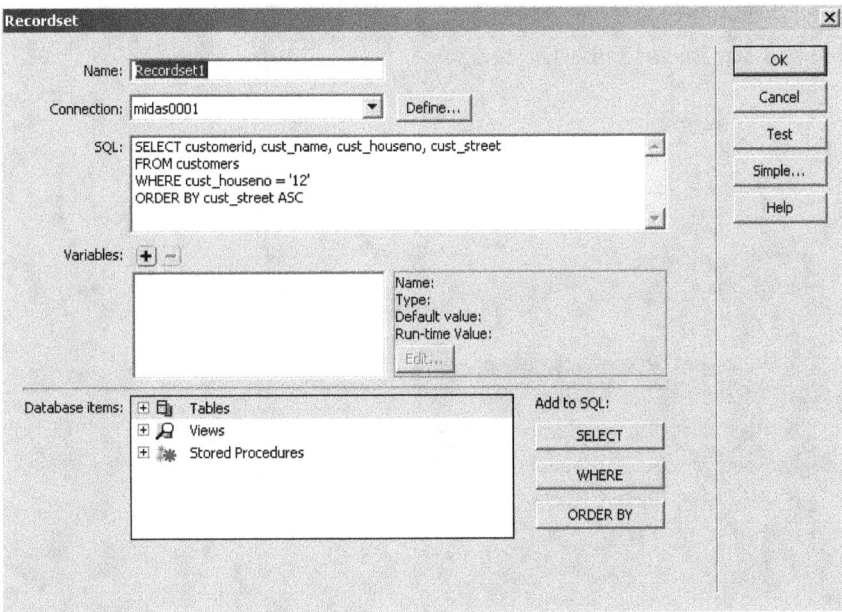

Figure 20

If you click on the Advanced button you will see a dialogue window that you will use quite frequently. See Figure 20. DreamWeaver has converted the selected drop down menus in to real MySQL code. As you learn to create your own MySQL code you will find, that the simple recordset dialogue window is very limited. You will eventually create more complex MySQL code in phpmyadmin and then test it in DreamWeaver to ensure that it works well on your page. It is a good idea to have shortcuts/favorites in your web browser to your localhost page, phpmyadmin and your web page index. You will create new tables and columns in phpmyadmin regularly and will have to switch back and forth to DreamWeaver quite often. Don't forget to always refresh the Bindings tab in DreamWeaver (see Figure 21) to see your new database entries. Every time you save your file DreamWeaver will save it to your root folder and your testing/remote folder.

Figure 21

This is what your MySQL code may look like in your PHP page. The MySQL code is held within your PHP code.

```
mysql_select_db($database_midas0001, $midas0001);
$query_Recordset1menubar = "SELECT * FROM pcclientlinks WHERE linkdisplay = 'yes' and page = 'clientindex' ORDER BY `order` ASC";
$Recordset1menubar = mysql_query($query_Recordset1menubar, $midas0001) or die(mysql_error());
$row_Recordset1menubar = mysql_fetch_assoc($Recordset1menubar);
$totalRows_Recordset1menubar = mysql_num_rows($Recordset1menubar);
```

If you have tested your MySQL code in phpmyadmin, then used DreamWeaver to add the code to your page, you will want to see this page run in your web browser. Remember to point your web browser at the following address https://localhost/mytestsite/yourfilenamehere.php

Now you are really using XAMPP; Apache will serve the page to your local host, PHP will interpret the PHP code and execute any necessary functions. Functions containing MySQL code will be executed by the MySQL server. PHP will access this data and then display it on your web page.

12 RESOLVING PAGE ERRORS

Errors do occur, but thankfully they are displayed in the web page and even inform you which line of code is wrong. If you make an error with the naming convention of your MySQL database, tables or columns this will be displayed in your web page too.

Use Google to help you locate common errors; it is an invaluable tool at your disposal. Remember many people have used XAMPP over the years and chances are they have had the same issue or problem, too. You can use the MySQL web site documentation to help you with writing your SQL queries; it's another great tool to assisting you in achieving your goal.

YouTube has great tutorials to help you with developing your web site. Don't look at it as time wasting; you are learning and slowly understanding what you can do and what you can't do by example. There are great sites on the web with an answer to every question you have. Don't take the first answer as correct and written in stone. Check as many answers as you can so you can see a pattern of correctness. Once you have learnt it, you won't forget it. If you do forget the answer, you sure will know how to find it again.

There are times when the answer doesn't seem forthcoming; so, join PHP code forums and MySQL forums; there are some really great people out there that have the answers and are only too happy to help. Be polite at all times and you will get your answer. Remember that everyone has a way of doing things – that includes you! Most important of all, be patient, explain yourself as best as you can. Provide software versions with your questions, as some times software can have issues that you were not aware of.

The Internet is global, I have had to wait overnight for responses to questions, and so patience is the key to getting your answers.

I have tried numerous tools to help me with the development of my systems, but to be honest, DreamWeaver, XAMPP and backup software are the ones I use the most. Remember you are not the first person to have thought about your idea; there will be many similar ideas out there. Don't be afraid to examine web pages to see how things are done. Simply right click on the web page, select 'View Source' and it will display most of the page's code. There are plenty of third party applications, known as DreamWeaver Extensions that can simplify the process of building web sites. Hunt them down; spending an hour researching software can save you days if not weeks of development frustration.

13 CHOOSING A HOSTING SERVER

You're going to need a Linux hosting server that will allow you to upload your MySQL database and your PHP files. There are plenty of hosting companies out there with variable prices, so have a good look round.

You will need to know how your database system is going to be used; how many users will be interacting with it, and if they all need usernames and passwords. How often will they be accessing your system? Does the speed of the server matter to you or your users? How many online databases do you actually need? These are all important questions that need answering before you commit yourself to one particular hosting company.

Will you use a shared server or do you need a dedicated server? If you use a shared server the price will be very small per month, but the speed may be slow due to many other web sites on the system. There may be web shops and forums that are heavily used and these will affect the speed at which your users connect to your web site. A dedicated server is expensive, but it will allow you to have unlimited databases and unlimited connected users. You won't be sharing the server with other web sites, so access to your web site will be much, much quicker.

Once you have your server set up, you will have to create an online address, this is usually known as a domain name ending with .com, .org, .net. Most server providers will set this up for you and you simply pay an annual fee to keep the address for yourself.

Now you will be able to create your first online database using the wizards provided by your hosting company. Your database will be created with a number value similar to the following db435881388. This is not at all like the name of the database you have on your system, but it will still work once you understand what to do. You will need to export your database from your local phpmyadmin system. You can save this exported data as a file or copy and paste it into your online database. Once your hosting company has created your database, you should be able to click on it and see that they are using phpmyadmin, too. This makes life much easier because you will now be familiar with phpmyadmin. You can import your data from the file you created or you can paste your data in via the SQL query field.

You may get an error because you are using a different version of phpmyadmin than your hosting company, but it is easy resolved following the on screen prompts.

14 USING FTP

FTP stands for file transfer protocol, in simple terms it will help you to upload and download your files from a web server. Using your hosting company's FTP wizard will allow you to create a directory to store your PHP files in. Remember to name this exactly the same as your local site folder. Once you have uploaded your files to the new directory, you will need to edit the Connections/mynewdatabase.php (see Figure 17) file and add your online details, they will look something like the following.

```php
<?php
# FileName="Connection_php_mysql.htm"
# Type="MYSQL"
# HTTP="true"
$hostname_mydb = "localhost:/tmp/mysql5.sock";
$database_mydb = " db435881388";
$username_ mydb = " dbo435881388";
$password_ mydb = "password";
$ mydb = mysql_pconnect($hostname_ mydb, $username_ mydb,
$password_ mydb) or trigger_error(mysql_error(),E_USER_ERROR);
?>
```

You will now be able to type your full domain address in the browser and see your live web page. If there is a problem connecting to the database, don't worry its not broken. The error should tell you which file is causing the problem. It's usually the database names and passwords that are the culprits so check the details on your hosting server to verify all the details are correct.

Now that your online web site is fully functional you can add the online host details to DreamWeaver, which will synchronies your localhost with your remote host. If you are still updating your MySQL database on your local host, don't forget you will have to update it online too, or you will get errors appearing on your live web page.

15 BACKING UP YOUR WORK

Having come this far, the last thing you want is for all your work to be lost due to some virus, computer crash or silly DreamWeaver mistake. DreamWeaver allows you to skip certain files during the synchronization process. This is known as 'cloaking' and is found in the Advanced Site Definition dialogue window. See Figure 22. Your connections file on your local host (see Figure 23) will be very different than your connections file online (see previous page). You will need to make sure that DreamWeaver does not overwrite one file with the other. These are more reasons for backing up your work regularly.

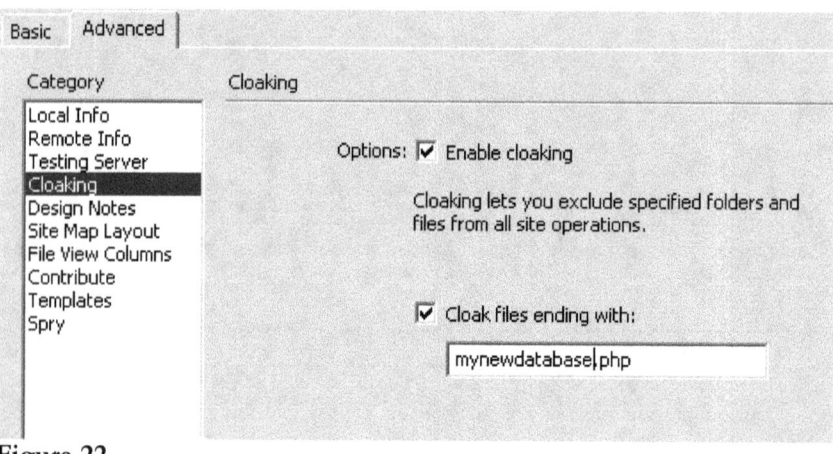

Figure 22

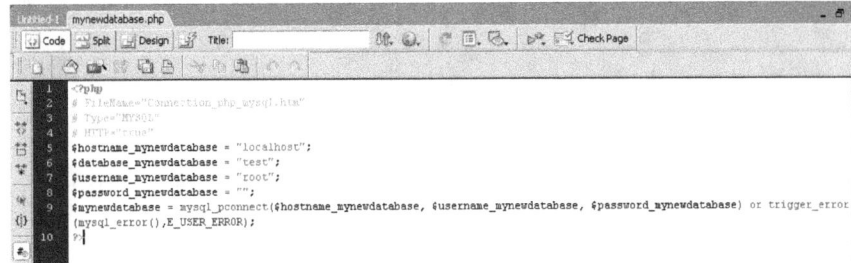

```php
<?php
# FileName="Connection_php_mysql.htm"
# Type="MYSQL"
# HTTP="true"
$hostname_mynewdatabase = "localhost";
$database_mynewdatabase = "test";
$username_mynewdatabase = "root";
$password_mynewdatabase = "";
$mynewdatabase = mysql_pconnect($hostname_mynewdatabase, $username_mynewdatabase, $password_mynewdatabase) or trigger_error
(mysql_error(),E_USER_ERROR);
?>
```

Figure 23

16 COBIAN BACKUP

A great little back up application is Cobian Backup. Check it out here http://www.cobian.se/index.htm. You can set the backups so they run automatically each day. You can also ask it to back up individual files as well as folders. Best of all the backups are zipped up so you can easily access them with WinZip. It's a clever little program that sits in your task bar. It can run automatically using a preset timer or you can simply right click and set the backup to run manually. See Figure 24.

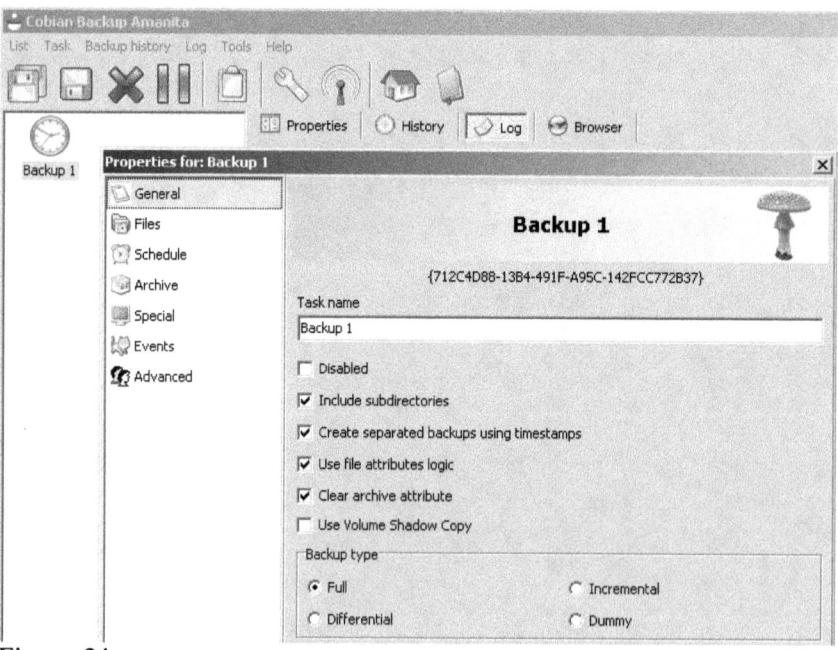

Figure 24

17 DUMPTIMER

Backing up all your PHP files is very important, but you also need to back up your database regularly, too. You could log in to your online hosting server, select the database and perform an export to file. This is okay, but would be time consuming and very much of a grind. I have several customers and each customer has their own database, and unique domain address, for security reasons. They use their database system for at least 16 hours a day. So creating a backup from each database every day would be simple enough. But I wanted my local databases to be copies or replicas of their online counterparts. This would mean me deleing the existing local database and then creating a new database from the backed up remote database.

After a lot of Internet searching I found the program to solve my problem. DumpTimer, found here: http://www.dumptimer.com/, allows me to back up remote databases and restore them in my local MySQL folder. See Figure 25.
I can now work on the very latest customer data without affecting the customer's live system. The software automatically runs every few hours, then I use the Cobian Backup software to save all the data to a compressed zip file.

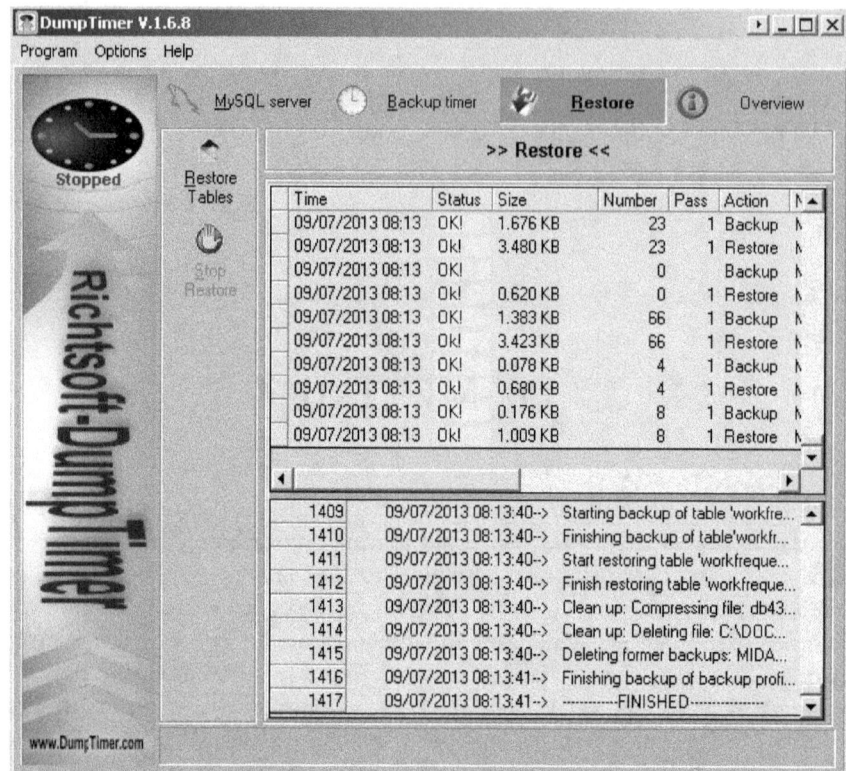

Figure 25

18 CUTE FTP PRO

DreamWeaver has its own built in FTP software that synchronizes your local folder with your remote folder. This is pretty good when you have just a few files, but when you have hundreds of files it becomes rather slow and annoying, simply because it is checking every single file on the local host with every single file on the remote host.

The solution is software like Cute FTP Pro, found here http://www.cuteftp.com/cuteftp/. See Figure 26. It allows you to upload and download files as well as view and edit files. This software allows you to upload individual files without the time consuming synchronizations of DreamWeaver. Unfortunately Cute FTP Pro is not free, although you can use the latest version of FileZilla for free found here https://wiki.filezilla-project.org/FileZilla_Client_Tutorial_%28en%29.

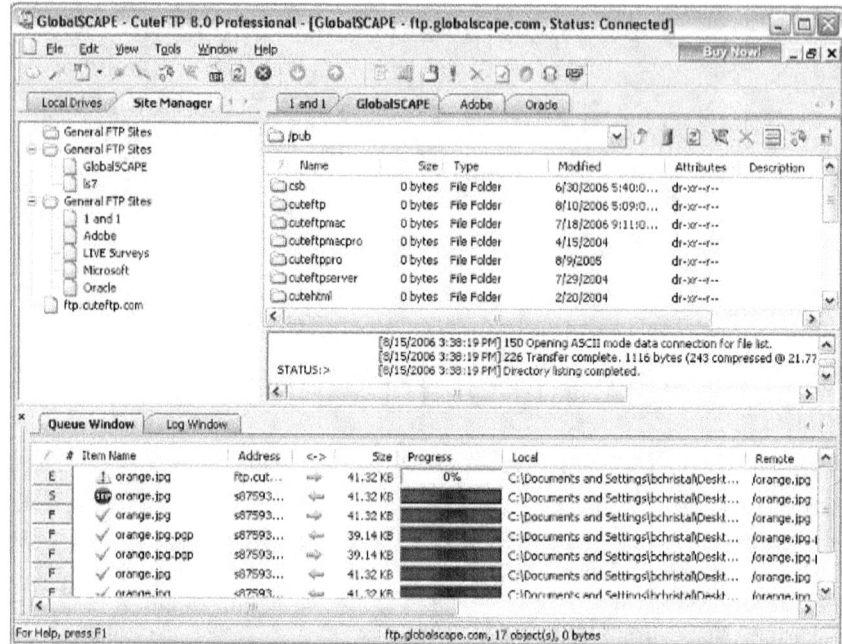

Figure 26

19 TOAD FOR MYSQL

There are times when you need to view tables and columns in a certain way. For example, you may want to compare two individual databases and unfortunately phpmyadmin doesn't quite do it as good as Toad for MySQL from Quest Software. You can download it from here http://www.toadworld.com/m/freeware/552.aspx. See Figure 27. Why would you want to compare two databases, you may well ask. If you have made quite a few changes to your local database to improve speed and efficiency, and all runs well on your local host you may decide to update the remote database with these changes. By comparing the two databases side by side, Toad is able to show you quite clearly what changes you need to make. You can also use Toad in the same way as you would use phpmyadmin, and best of all its free!

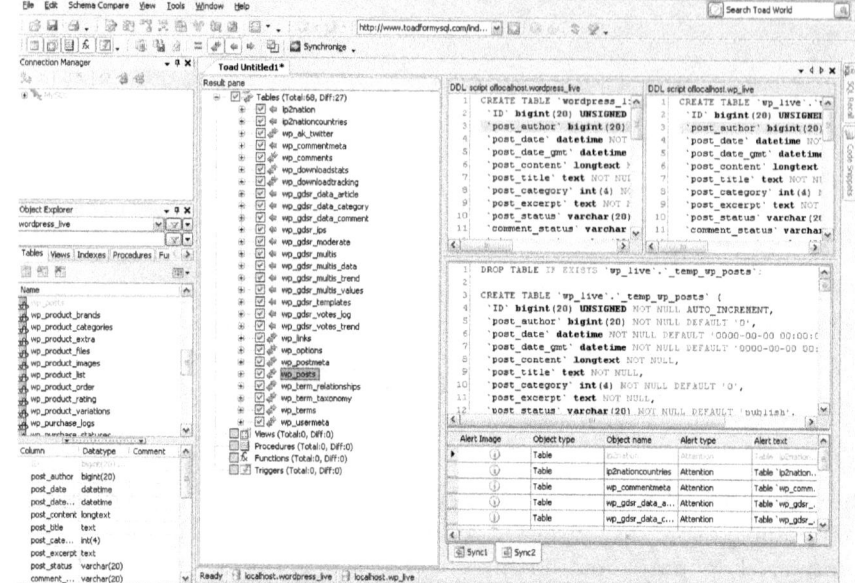

Figure 27

20 XAMPP AND MULTIPLE DOMAINS

You can have multiple folders within your XAMPP/htdocs folder and access them by typing localhost/myfolder/index.php into your browser address bar. This is a simple method so you don't have to edit any of the XAMPP files installed. If, however, you want to set up a Virtual Host, myhost/mywebsite/index.PHP, to allow additional users access to the files held in a specific directory, you will need to edit the XAMPP configuration files.

Open the XAMPP control panel, click on the Apache config button and select the Browse [Apache] link. The Apache folder will appear, then open the 'conf' folder and then the 'extra' folder. Finally, open the document called httpd-vhosts.conf add all the following text starting from <VirtualHost *:80> to </VirtualHost> to the bottom of the file.

```
<VirtualHost *:80>
        ServerAdmin webmaster@localhost
        DocumentRoot "C:/XAMPP/mywebsite/"
        ServerName testproject
        ErrorLog "logs/mywebsite-error.log"
        CustomLog "logs/mywebsite-access.log" common
        <Directory "c:/XAMPP/mywebsite/">
                Options Indexes FollowSymLinks Includes ExecCGI
                AllowOverride All
                #insert this line
                Require all granted
                #end insertion
        </Directory>
</VirtualHost>
```

Don't forget to save it. We now need to edit the 'host' file located at C:\WINDOWS\system32\drivers\etc and add the following details. Remember when changing the Host file you may have to restart your computer for Windows to accept the new changes. If you delete an address from the local host, you will have to restart your computer for Windows to acknowledge these changes.

127.0.0.1   mywebsite.com

Now we need to create the directory that our new virtual server will be using inside the XAMPP folder. Name the folder mywebsite.
We really need to put something in the folders to verify that the server is accessing the correct directory. Create a text file in the directory and name it index.PHP, then enter the following PHP code.

```
<pre><?PHP print_r($_SERVER); ?></pre>
```

Now turn off the Apache server for a minute or so by using the XAMPP control panel. Once the server is up and running again, enter the following into your browser's address bar: http://mywebsite.com/. Your virtual server should be up and running. If you want multiple servers, just repeat the process above.

21 MAKING XAMPP MORE SECURE

XAMPP offers built in security that you can add quite easily. If you are using XAMPP and your desktop computer is connected to a number of other computers, then it would be wise to add some form of security. If you are going to use XAMPP as a public server then you really must add security. From the localhost screen click on the 'Security' link and the following page will appear. Then click on the link, displayed, as shown in Figure 28.

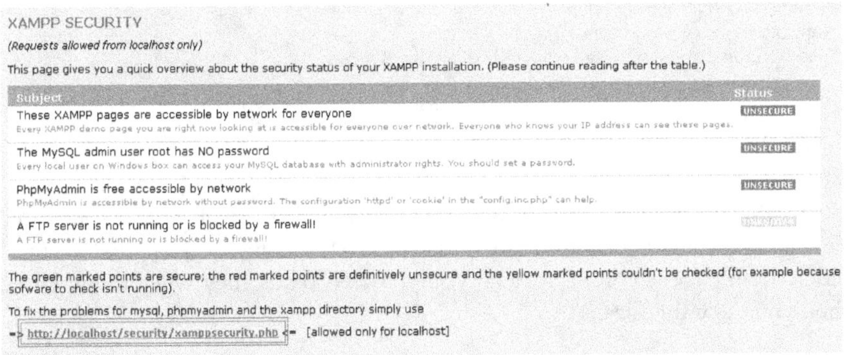

Figure 28

Once you change the root password, XAMPP will confirm this and you will need to restart the MySQL server using the XAMPP control panel. See Figure 29.

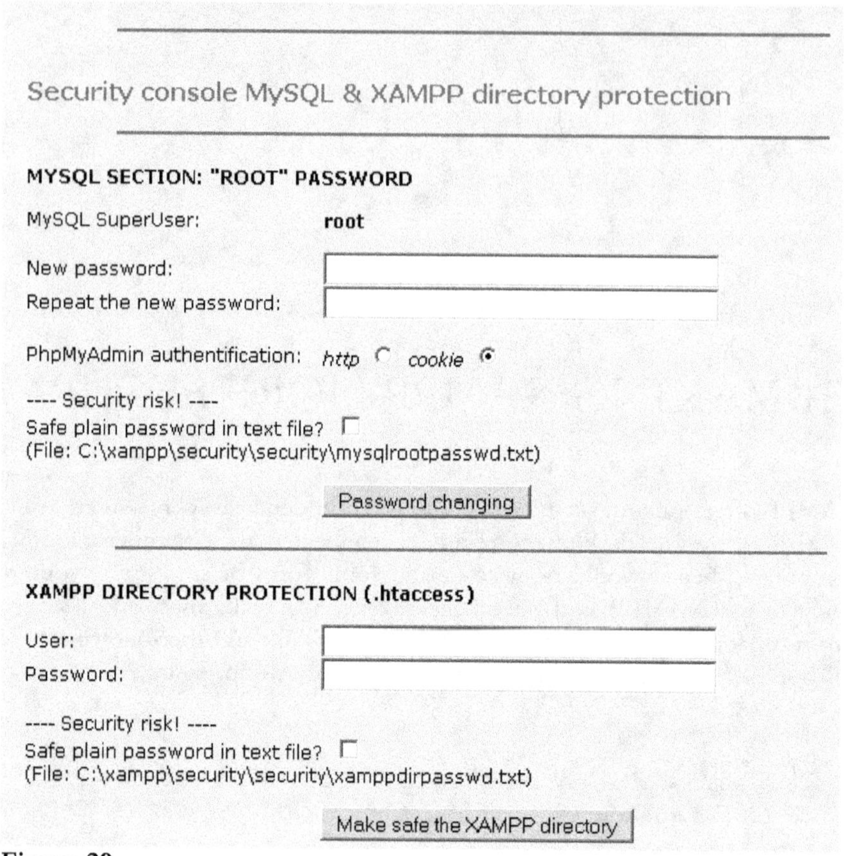

Security console MySQL & XAMPP directory protection

MYSQL SECTION: "ROOT" PASSWORD

MySQL SuperUser: **root**

New password:

Repeat the new password:

PhpMyAdmin authentification: *http* ○ *cookie* ◉

---- Security risk! ----
Safe plain password in text file? ☐
(File: C:\xampp\security\security\mysqlrootpasswd.txt)

Password changing

XAMPP DIRECTORY PROTECTION (.htaccess)

User:

Password:

---- Security risk! ----
Safe plain password in text file? ☐
(File: C:\xampp\security\security\xamppdirpasswd.txt)

Make safe the XAMPP directory

Figure 29

After entering the new user and password, XAMPP displays the following. See Figure 30. You can find the passwords stored in the XAMPP security folder. Don't forget NOT to lose your passwords as they will be encrypted when you view the files.

SUCCESS: The XAMPP directory is protected now! All personal data was safed in the following file:
C:\xampp\security\xampp.users
C:\xampp\htdocs\xampp\.htaccess

Figure 30

Now that you have secured XAMPP, when you click on the Security link again you will find that XAMPP confirms this as seen in Figure 31. Now when we decide to use phpmyadmin we will need to enter a password as seen in Figure 32 to gain access. If you try to access the localhost folder, you will find that it is secured as well and requires a password to view the pages, see Figure 33.

Subject	Status
These XAMPP pages are no longer accessible by network for everyone	SECURE
The MySQL admin user root has no longer no password	SECURE
PhpMyAdmin password login is enabled.	SECURE
A FTP server is not running or is blocked by a firewall!	UNKNOWN
A FTP server is not running or is blocked by a firewall!	

Figure 31

phpMyAdmin

Welcome to phpMyAdmin

Language

English ▾

Log in

Username:

Password:

Go

Figure 32

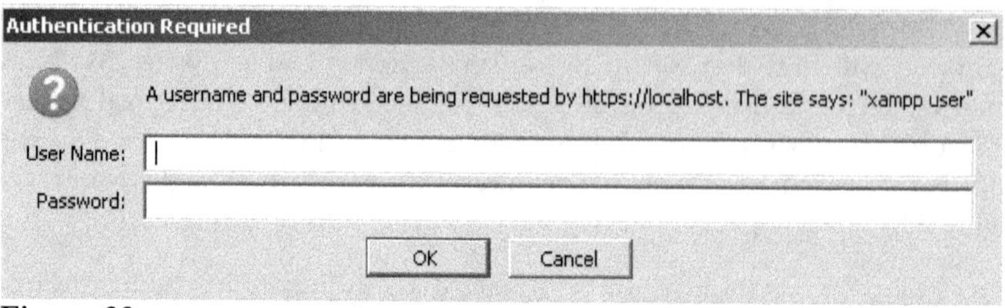
Authentication Required
A username and password are being requested by https://localhost. The site says: "xampp user"
User Name:
Password:
OK
Cancel

Figure 33

22 SECURING YOUR VIRTUAL SERVER

The htaccess file provides security at folder level for the Apache server. If you want to protect your virtual host directories you need to create a .htaccess file and a .htpasswd file in the root directory of your virtual server folders. Add the following details to the .htaccess file:

AuthType Basic
AuthName "My Protected Area"
AuthUserFile /path/to/.htpasswd
Require valid-user

The password for the .htpasswd file needs to be encrypted for security reasons. Visit the site HTACCESSTOOLS by going to the following address http://www.htaccesstools.com/htpasswd-generator-windows/
Once you enter your username and password in the fields provided, the web site will generate your encrypted password similar to the following.
billray1970:$apr1$PEl3kYSj$eGZL4wUZj5T73EbjHt6nQ.
You will need to add these details to your .htpasswd file and save them.
To create a dot prefix file open note pad, select File, Save As, then add the file name .htaccess and select Save as type: All Files, and click Save. Don't forget to restart the XAMPP server to ensure the security works correctly. When you try and access your virtual server you should see a dialog box similar to Figure 33.

23 XAMPP AND THE INTERNET

There may come a time when you want to access your local host via the Internet. Maybe you have a web site that you want to show others, or you may have even built a dynamic system that you want to test through the Internet. Whatever the reason, you will have to make XAMPP, your local host server, available to the Internet. You should have a router that connects your computer to the Internet. The router is very important as it protects your computer from the perils that exist on the Internet – viruses, malware, spyware, etc. To allow XAMPP to be visible to the WWW, we need to add a Port Forwarding address to the router's settings. This will just allow port 80 to be available to the Internet, leaving your other ports out of harm's way. Remember to follow all the security recommendations in the previous chapter before you set up Port Forwarding.

Get the gateway address found in your control panel under local area connection. You will need the IP Address and the Default Gateway Address. See figure 34.

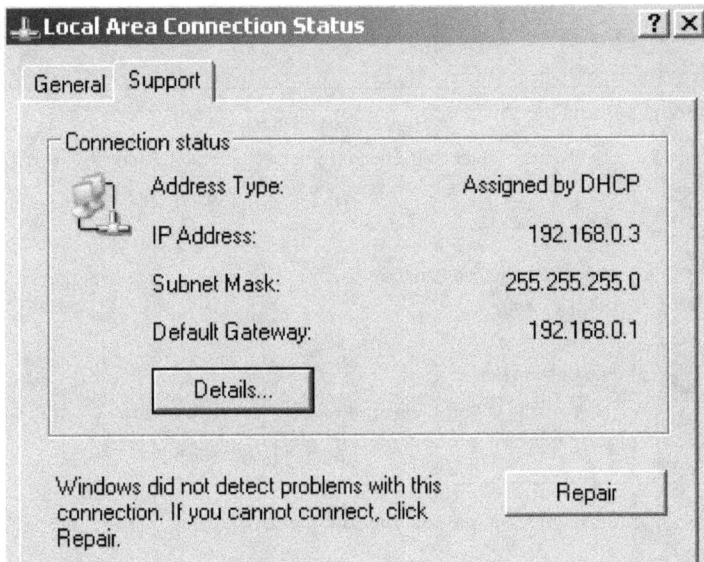

Figure 34

If you enter the Gateway Address in to your browser you will see a dialog window similar to Figure 33. This gateway address is actually a connection to your router and will require a password to access the router settings. If you're not sure what your router password is, try the following web site on the Internet as it covers all the numerous router manufacturers around the world.

http://www.default-password.info/.

If that doesn't help, try typing in the name of your router and the model number in to Google, you're bound to find the password and username that way.

Once you're logged in to the router settings, you need to look for a link or heading that says 'Port Forwarding'. See Figure 35. You need to enter the port number 80 as this is the port your local host is available from. You will also need your local IP address, so that the router knows which computer to allow a connection to, see Figure 34.

Your router application my look similar to Figure 35.

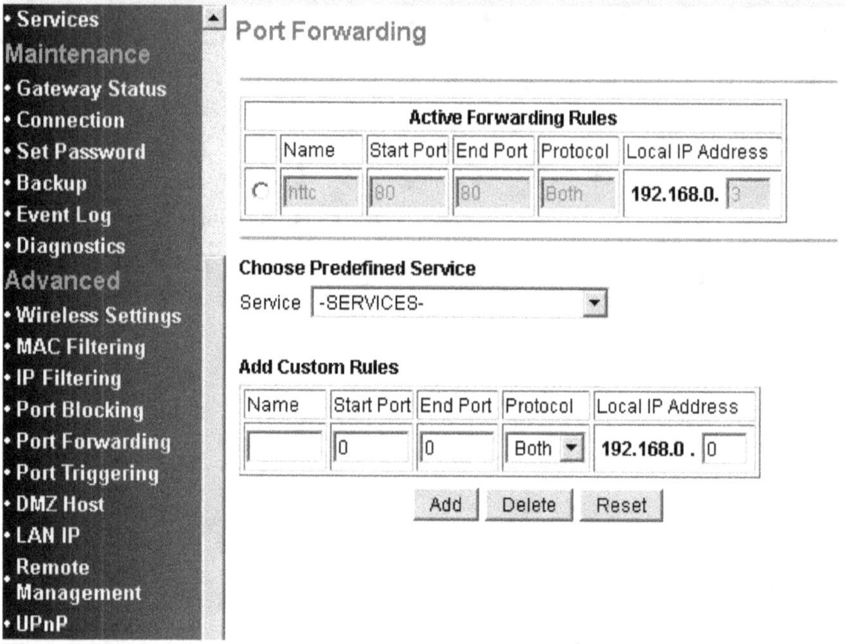

- Services
Maintenance
- Gateway Status
- Connection
- Set Password
- Backup
- Event Log
- Diagnostics
Advanced
- Wireless Settings
- MAC Filtering
- IP Filtering
- Port Blocking
- Port Forwarding
- Port Triggering
- DMZ Host
- LAN IP
- Remote Management
- UPnP

Port Forwarding

Active Forwarding Rules

	Name	Start Port	End Port	Protocol	Local IP Address
○	http	80	80	Both	192.168.0. 3

Choose Predefined Service

Service -SERVICES- ▼

Add Custom Rules

Name	Start Port	End Port	Protocol	Local IP Address
	0	0	Both ▼	192.168.0 . 0

Add   Delete   Reset

Figure 35

Once you have entered these new details, remember to click save. You now need to find out what your remote IP address is. This is the address that the World Wide Web will use to access your web site. Head over to http://myipaddress.com and copy the four sets of digits and paste them into your web browser address bar and press the enter key. If you have the XAMPP servers running correctly, you should now see your web page fully functional. Why not try and enter the same remote IP address in your smart phone browser, you should see the same page, only smaller.

24 USING PERL

Perl is a server side programming language; it was known as the duct tape of the Internet and is as old as the Internet. It is used for text processing, accessing databases, CGI programming, low and high-level applications and much, much more. XAMPP has a Perl module included that allows you to write Perl scripts, place them in your htdocs folder and view the executed code in your browser. You could write your web page using Perl instead of PHP, but PHP is the most popular language and is used by most web hosting companies. PHP has database functionality built in, especially for MySQL; unfortunately Perl doesn't. Pearl has Internet functionality bolted on whereas PHP was made specifically for the Internet. PHP is easier to use, faster and more secure. Why not visit http://w3techs.com/ to see the overall usage of PHP compared to Perl. You can also see how popular the Apache Server is too, see Figure 36.

A Perl script looks like the following…

```
#!"C:\xampp\perl\bin\perl.exe"
use CGI;
$co = new CGI;
print $co->header,
$co->start_html('CGI Example'),
$co->center('welcome to CGI'),
$co->end_html;
```

Server-side Programming Languages

Most popular server-side programming languages

© W3Techs.com	usage	change since 1 June 2013
1. PHP	80.5%	+0.4%
2. ASP.NET	19.5%	-0.4%
3. Java	2.8%	-0.2%
4. ColdFusion	0.9%	
5. Perl	0.7%	

percentages of sites

Fastest growing server-side programming languages since 1 June 2013

© W3Techs.com	sites
1. PHP	966
2. JavaScript	6
3. Lasso	1

daily number of additional sites
in the top 10 million

Figure 36

25 A FINAL NOTE

Picking the best tools to do a job is always going to be difficult, but if you follow the trend of popularity you will always be better off. The more popular a language becomes, the more knowledge that becomes available, which is what you need when things go wrong. There will be many more answers to your queries, and not all of them will be correct. You will find many more examples of code, hints and tips; some that work well and some that don't.

The Internet is your tool bag; it's a box of tricks with everything that you need to help you build a better web site. Don't forget too, that employers are always using the most popular languages, and they pay well for good programmers. You have taken the first steps to learning PHP and MySQL; and XAMPP is your starting block. A simple understanding of XAMPP will help you understand why errors occur in your PHP and MySQL code and how to solve them.

I hope you have learnt how to get the best out of this amazing software system. I'm sure you will save hours of frustrating searches as well as hours of your development time. By simply following the basic guidelines that I have provided, will make you more aware and understanding of what is going on under the XAMPP hood.

John Henderson